re:act:

For the tough times

does God care when I'm hurting?

Kate Hayes

**small group Bible resources from
Scripture Union**

FOR THE TOUGH TIMES

Published by Scripture Union, 207–209 Queensway, Bletchley, MK2 2EB, England.

Scripture Union: We are an international Christian charity working with churches in more than 130 countries providing resources to bring the good news about Jesus Christ to children, young people and families – and to encourage them to develop spiritually through the Bible and prayer. As well as our network of volunteers, staff and associates who run holidays, church-based events and school Christian groups, we produce a wide range of publications and support those who use our resources through training programmes.

Email: info@scriptureunion.org.uk
Internet: http://www.scriptureunion.org.uk

© Copyright Kate Hayes 2002

First published 2002

ISBN 1 85999 622 1

All rights reserved. No part of this publication may be reproduced, stored in a retrieval system, or transmitted, in any form or by any means, electronic, mechanical, photocopying, recording or otherwise, without the prior permission of Scripture Union.

The right of Kate Hayes to be identified as author of this work has been asserted by her in accordance with the Copyright, Designs and Patents Act 1988.

Scripture taken from the *New Living Translation*, British text, published by Tyndale House Publishers, Inc, Wheaton, Illinois, USA, and distributed by STL Ltd, Carlisle, Cumbria, England; and from *The Message* © Eugene H Peterson, used by permission of NavPress Publishing Group.

Extracts from *A Grief Observed* by C S Lewis, published by Faber and Faber Ltd, are used with permission.

British Library Cataloguing-in-Publication Data: a catalogue record for this book is available from the British Library.

Cover design and photography by David Lund Design, Milton Keynes.

Illustrations by Helen Gale.

Printed and bound in Great Britain by Ebenezer Baylis & Son Ltd, The Trinity Press, London Road, Worcester WR5 2JH.

Contents

Welcome! 4

Intro 6

1: Preview 8

2: When the going gets tough 12

3: Why me? 17

4: When darkness falls 23

5: Facing pain 29

6: God's response 35

7: But it still hurts 41

Welcome to **re:action** discussion guides for small groups!

What are the distinctives of **re:action**? The series is strong on links into the contemporary world and concerned that God's Word impacts our everyday lives in practical ways. Understanding the truth leads to a response in the heart and mind of the individual. The sessions encourage personal discovery through actively exploring the Bible but, unlike many group Bible studies on the market, **re:action** assumes little if any prior Bible knowledge. As such it is excellent for those new to looking at Christianity, but that is not to say that the series is lightweight or lacking in depth. More mature Christians will find the series refreshing. The quality of questions should produce lively and thinking debate, and opportunities to share personal experiences. Though some humour is used, especially in the icebreaker **set the scene** sections, the content of the sessions overall is demanding and personally challenging.

Kate Hayes began writing the series out of a sense of frustration with existing materials, and everything she produces has been tried and tested in her own church groups. She says: 'Most study notes are frankly boring. Too many work on a 'the answer must be Jesus' principle, regurgitating bits of text for answers. Others don't seem to relate the learning so as to make a difference to people's everyday lives. I don't write these notes because I want people to find answers to academic questions or clock up the books they've studied and then move on to something else, but because I want to see people grow in understanding and maturity. I want them to find out things that will make a difference every day of their lives, when work is tough, when friends let them down, their lives fall apart and they're faced with living as Christians in our postmodern society.'

Each title in the series contains material for seven sessions. **Preview** is an introductory session that ideally would take place in a social setting, perhaps following a potluck supper or around desserts and coffee. Each session begins with **set the scene**, a light discussion opener, sometimes in the form of a quiz or game, or some fun questions. The **explore** section takes the group into the Bible text, while the **reflect** section moves into the area of personal application. Note that while most of the questions are for group discussion, there are also periods of quiet for tackling personal questions, which don't have to be shared more widely. In the closing `re:action` section there is opportunity to pray through what's been discussed and discovered, and sometimes suggestions for other actions both within and outside the group times.

What about leadership of the group? The `re:action` series is aimed at thinking people willing to be pro-active in searching the Scriptures and discussing their implications. As such, the leadership of the group, by one or two members, can be run with a light touch. The role of the `re:action` group leader is that of a guide through the discussion material rather than a teacher. The leader will sensitively encourage the sharing of answers and personal experiences at an appropriate level. Many questions need just one word answers and can be moved through quite quickly; at other times some brainstorming of ideas would be an appropriate response to the questions; sometimes it will be a more measured and thoughtful discussion. The leader will need to make decisions about when tangents to the discussion are legitimate and when they distract.

Ideally everyone should have their own copy of the booklet and follow through the material together. It's essential for everyone to bring a Bible, as much of the time will be spent around open Bibles. Any translation is fine, and it's often useful to compare different versions. For those new to Bible study, several contemporary translations are to be recommended: the Good News Bible, the Contemporary English Version, or the New Living Translation – and it's the NLT which is used in the booklet whenever Bible text is quoted. It will be useful to have a supply of pens, paper and perhaps card available.

About the author

Kate Hayes, born into a non-churchgoing family in Sheffield, decided to become a Christian aged 12 after being 'dragged along' to a Pathfinder meeting by a friend. After studying Psychology she did teacher training but then found herself working in bookshops and in software testing for the book trade. In 1994 she moved to Dukinfield in Greater Manchester, where she now coordinates and writes materials for small groups in St John's Church.

Intro

In an episode of the BBC TV programme *Holby City*, the hospital chaplain found out he had a heart condition and might die during the operation to fix it. He asked God why he had allowed this to happen to him when he'd served him for so many years – and concluded that he no longer believed in God.

When people respond like this it seems that they have never thought through the reality of undeserved suffering. So when, inevitably, they finally come face to face with it, they have no means of coping.

The unexpected diagnosis... the latenight phone call... the shocking letter out of the blue... the unforeseen disaster... the unimaginable relationship breakdown... the split second collision of circumstances after which life will never be the same... One day – if not already – you will face the experience of undeserved suffering, in your own life or that of someone you love. Why me? Why them?

How can you prepare for that day? Are there no answers at all?

C S Lewis describes the feeling of having no answers for suffering in his book *A Grief Observed*, written after the death of his wife:

Where is God? ... Go to him when your need is desperate, when all other help is vain, and what do you find? A door slammed in your face, and a sound of bolting and double-bolting on the inside. After that, silence. You may as well turn away. The longer you wait, the more emphatic the silence will become... Why is he so very absent a help in time of trouble?

It's time to learn from a story written thousands of years ago – the Old Testament book of Job. You don't need a history or a theology degree to get a great deal out of looking at Job's story. Who was he? If his name is known at all it's as a byword for suffering and patience. But there's pretty much nothing known about him beyond an opening description in the first chapter of the book – as a wealthy, good-living, God-fearing man. The author is unknown, as is the time of writing and the time of Job himself, and the location of Uz can only be put as 'somewhere in the Middle East'!

for the tough times

But in spite of all we don't know about Job, we do know that his story concerns one of the biggest issues men and women ever wrestle with — how can we cope with the really tough times?

1 Preview

*I have no peace, no quietness.
I have no rest; instead, only trouble comes.*

Job 3:26

set the scene

What would you like to know about others in the group? Without getting too deep and meaningful (such as: what do you think is the secret of a successful life?) everyone should to write down a question they'd like someone else in the group to answer. For example:

Q: What made you start coming to our church?

Q: What's your favourite breakfast?

Q: Have you ever played a musical instrument?

Put the questions into a dish or plastic sandwich box and pass it round the group. One at a time, draw out a question and answer it out loud (briefly!) before putting it back and passing the container on. Keep going until you've run out of time or had enough! If you draw the same question twice, then select another one.

explore

1 Being a Christian

Q: When did you become a Christian?

Some people may not be able to answer that question. Perhaps…

- you were brought up in a Christian family and can't remember a time when you didn't believe and trust in Jesus

for the tough times

- you're not sure that you are a Christian
- growing to know Jesus happened over a long period of time and you can't put a date to it

Q: If you can remember becoming a Christian, what made you become a Christian when you did?

Q: Why didn't you do it before?

Discuss the kinds of things that put someone off becoming a Christian. Sometimes people have good reasons for not taking steps in that direction. They have real questions and doubts that they want sorted first. Sometimes the arguments are only red herrings; they really aren't interested at all.

2 Asking questions about Christianity

Q: What kind of questions and problems do you find people have about Christianity and being a Christian?

Q: If someone asks you a really complicated question about being a Christian, what are you most likely to do?
- give them the phone number of your vicar/pastor/housegroup leader/best friend/worst enemy?
- pretend you're about to be sick and run away?
- get out your Bible, your commentaries and every Christian book you've ever bought and spend six hours discussing it with them in great detail?
- babble something and pray that it makes sense to them!
- say, 'Oh, that's a good one. I'll have to think about that.' And hope they forget about it?
- change the subject?
- get back to them once you've thought about it a bit more?
- tell them they should stop worrying and just get on with things?

re:action

- something else? What?

Discuss your reactions in the group. It makes life much simpler if questions have straightforward answers, doesn't it! But sometimes there doesn't seem to be much of an answer at all. In Job we look at one of the biggest questions of all – one that definitely doesn't have an easy answer.

3 The problem of suffering

Read

Job 7:1–21

Q: Why do you think the issue of why people suffer causes so many problems?

In this passage, Job expresses his views on his suffering. Look through the passage and choose four words or phrases that you think sum up Job's feelings here.

1
2
3
4

Suffering can shut out almost everything good in life; it isn't just about feeling a bit low or having a bad hair day. Job says that suffering can be immensely painful (v11) and scary (v14). It can seem as though nothing will ever be good again (v7). It can make us feel that life isn't worth living if this is all there is (v15,16). It can leave us feeling that God has singled us out for punishment (v20).

Why does God allow suffering? There don't seem to be any simple answers to this question but we aren't left to struggle without any help at all. In Job, and in other parts of the Bible, we find help to face, and make some sense of, the suffering that is an inevitable part of our lives and the lives of those around us.

reflect

Spend a few minutes thinking through these next questions on your own first.

for the tough times

Q: How do you usually handle life's unexpected difficulties or struggles?

Q: Are you happy with the way you cope? Can you recall a particular problem that you handled really well?

Q: Is there anything in your reaction to suffering, pain or difficulty that you would rather do without? Can you recall any time of struggle when, looking back now, you think you could have done better?

Now share as much or as little of your thoughts with the rest of the group as you are comfortable with.

re:action

Discuss as a group what insights or help you will be looking for as you look into Job together. Someone might like to **note** these down for review at the end of the sessions.

Pray for each other, particularly in areas of difficulty already mentioned.

Pray for others outside the group known to be suffering at the moment. If you aren't very confident praying aloud then just say the person's name aloud and silently ask God to bless or help or heal or strengthen or comfort. After each name and half a minute of silence the whole group could say together, 'Lord, please bless Jenny' or another simple and suitable sentence.

Pray together about your hopes for the group, allowing everyone to contribute as they wish, openly or privately.

During these studies we won't be reading every chapter of Job, as it is a long book. However, you may find it helpful to read through the whole book on your own before you next meet, or read it in sections over the next six weeks. Since the language in Job can be hard, consider using a newer version of the Bible such as the *Contemporary English Version*, *The Message* (an American paraphrase rather than a translation) or the *New Living Translation*. Bible verses printed in the **re:action** series come from the NLT.

2 When the going gets tough

Should we accept only good things from the hand of God and never anything bad?
Job 2:10

set the scene

Imagine you could plan anything you liked for tomorrow. All your commitments are taken care of and cost is no object. Share together/ discuss your answers to these questions:

Q: What would you do with the day?

Q: How would you hope to feel after a day like that?

Back to reality. What about today?

Q: Would you describe today as good, bad or indifferent? Why?

explore

Read
Job 1:1–5

Q: Which of these describe Job? Circle those you agree with.

| holy | wealthy | evil | prayerful | powerful |
| out of step with God | | drunkard | lazy | good |

1 A really, really bad day

Read
Job 1:13–22 and 2:7–10

for the tough times

Q: How would you sum up the four devastating messages that came to Job?
1
2
3
4

Q: Then, as if that wasn't enough, what else went wrong for him?

2 Behind the scenes

Read

Job 1:6–12 and 2:1–6

Now for a number of important questions. Work through them as a group.

Q: Who caused Job's suffering?

Q: Why did Satan want to attack Job?

Q: Why do you think God didn't stop Satan?

Q: Do you think people sometimes deserve the suffering that comes their way?

Q: Did God think Job deserved what happened to him?

Q: How do you feel about the way Job was treated?

re:action

3 Responding to disaster

Christians or not, people often blame God when things go wrong.

Q: Can you think of a time when you have done this yourself, or seen someone else do it?

Q: Why do you think people do this?

Think back to the disasters that happened to Job.

Q: How did he react to them? (1:20–22 and 2:8–10)

Q: Why did he respond like this?

Q: How did his wife react? (2:9)

Q: Why do you think she responded so differently?

Q: If you had been there, do you think you would have sided with Job or with his wife?

reflect

Imagine something wonderful has happened to you. Perhaps you've got that job you've always wanted, or passed that incredibly difficult exam or been left a thousand pounds in a great aunt's will…

Q: How do you feel? And how would you celebrate?

Another day. This time something awful has happened to you. Perhaps you've been made redundant from that perfect job or failed an exam

for the tough times

you can't retake or lost a thousand pounds and no one's handed it in…

Q: How do you feel now? And how would you try to cope?

Think about these two different kinds of days.

Q: What would you be most likely to do?

- Thank God for the good things but ignore him in the bad.
- Pray for help in the bad things but ignore him in the good.
- Spend as much time thanking him for the good things as praying for help in the bad.
- Spend more time in prayer over one than the other.
- Something else: what?

Discuss your reaction with the group before moving onto the next question.

Q: How do you explain your reaction?

Now some questions to reflect on in silence on your own. Take five minutes of quiet.

Q: What can go wrong when we cut God out of either the good or the bad moments of our lives?

Q: What good and what bad things are happening in your life at the moment?

Q: How could you share these things with God? Are you doing that?

re:action

Everyone in the group needs a sheet of paper. **Draw** a line vertically down the middle to make two columns. Put a large tick at the top of one side and a cross at the top of the other. Under the tick, **write down** some of the good things in your life that you could thank God for. Under the cross, **write down** some of the difficulties you face or needs you have. Spend a short time **sharing** some of these things together.

Pray together. Start by **thanking** God for the good things. You could do this by going round the group in turn with everyone either praying for or reading out one of the things they have written under their tick.

When everyone has had a turn, **read** Psalm 28:7 together:

The Lord is my strength, my shield from every danger.
 I trust in him with all my heart.
He helps me, and my heart is filled with joy.
 I burst out in songs of thanksgiving.

Pray again. Go round the group, this time praying for, or reading out, one of the things on the other column. This time, when everyone has had a turn, **read** Psalm 62:8 together:

O my people, trust in him at all times.
 Pour out your heart to him, for God is our refuge.

If you have space on your paper, you might like to **write these verses** on the appropriate halves and keep the paper where you will see it through the week ahead. Why not challenge one another to **memorise** the verses, so you can remind yourself of them when life is good and life is tough?

3 Why me?

Why have you made me your target?
Job 7:20

set the scene

Think back through your life. Hidden in the deepest recesses of your memory must be some 'why me?' kind of moments... those highly embarrassing or disastrous events which leave you wishing you were three thousand miles away or were thinking you should go out in disguise that day. Perhaps you suffer from 'foot in mouth' syndrome. Or you've always been clumsy, or forgetful, or maybe you just seem to attract disaster! It's time to confess. Discuss together your answers to the next two questions.

Q: What was your most embarrassing or disastrous experience?

Q: How do you feel when something like this happens to you? Why?

explore

Job's suffering

Four friends responded to Job's distress. These verses sum up much of what they said.

Read

Eliphaz: Job 4:7,8
Bildad: Job 8:20
Zophar: Job 11:14,15
Elihu: Job 34:11

Q: What did his friends see as the reason for Job's problems?

```
re:action
```

Many people believe that suffering is deserved in some way; something about the person or their actions is being punished. This belief is expressed in sayings such as 'as you sow, so shall you reap' and 'make your bed and lie in it'.

Read
John 9:1–3
Luke 13:1–5
Job 21:7–14

Q: What do these verses tell us about the causes of suffering?

Q: Do you think Job's friends were on the right track or not?

Job's friends remind us not to make assumptions about what has caused someone's suffering; there are several possible reasons. So, what does cause suffering? Here are some ideas to look at…

1 You and me

Track down a couple of newspapers from the past few weeks and look through them as a group.

Q: How many of the stories that hit the headlines involve suffering of some kind?

Cut out a selection of stories that catch your attention and divide them into two piles. Put all the stories where suffering was caused by something someone (that person or someone else) did or didn't do – 'through negligence, through weakness, through our own deliberate fault…' as the Anglican Communion service describes it – into one pile. In the second pile, put the stories where the suffering had some other cause.

Q: Which pile is the largest? Why do you think that is?

Reality check Some suffering is caused by you and me. All our actions have consequences and sometimes they can be destructive either to ourselves or others.

for the tough times

Next, in five minutes of silence, here are some questions to think about by yourself.

Q: Are you conscious of something you have done that caused hurt or damage to someone? Is there anything you can do about it now?

When we hurt someone it can leave us feeling very guilty. When someone hurts us we can be left with feelings of bitterness.

Q: When might such feelings become damaging to us?

We can ignore these feelings or dismiss them. We can hold onto them and allow them to take over our lives. Neither option seems very constructive.

2 Discipline

Read
Genesis 6:11–13
Acts 5:1–11
1 Corinthians 11: 27–30

Q: Why did the people in these passages suffer and/or die?

You may like to divide up into three groups and each look at one of the passages listed above, then report your findings to the others. Then extend your discussion to include thoughts on these extra verses:

Read

Hebrews 12:5,6,10,11

Persistent and unrepentant sin may lead to God's discipline but we can be sure he'll always tell us why if we ask him.

We should never assume that someone else is suffering as a result of God's discipline.

Time for another five minutes or so of quiet. And three questions for you to think about on your own:

re:action

Q: Are there things in your life that you know are wrong – yet you have not faced up to/attempted to end?

Q: Why might it be good to ask someone to help you do this?

Q: If you can see the value in asking for help, who could you ask?

3 Growing faith and understanding

Job's continuing faith in the face of disaster was important to two key characters:

- Satan – it proved to him that people did not necessarily follow God only for the good things they might receive.
- Job himself – he learnt just how strong his faith really was.

Q: Do you think Job would have felt differently about his suffering if he had known his response really mattered to God?

Q: Why do you think God didn't tell him?

The way we deal with tough times sometimes advances God's plans for us and for the world, although we may not always understand how.

Q: Do you agree with this statement?

4 Our fallen world

Read
Genesis 1:31
Genesis 3:22–24

Q: What was the world like when it was created?

for the tough times

Q: What changed things?

Reality check Once there was no sin, no death, no suffering. Sin brought disaster with it, and until the end of time we live with the consequences of our fallen, imperfect world. Suffering and hardship are a part of life.

reflect

Job did not know why he was suffering. We may have no idea why we are suffering either.

Q: Why do you think we want reasons for our suffering?

Q: Why is it so hard for us to live without them?

Job's suffering tested his faith in God to the limit but he held onto his belief that, whatever happened to him, God was still worth following and trusting.

Q: How much does your faith and trust in God depend on receiving good things from him?

re:action

Read this old hymn together, or **sing** it if enough people know the tune. Read/sing slowly so that you can think about the meaning:

Be Thou my Vision, O Lord of my heart;
Naught be all else to me, save that Thou art –
Thou my best thought, by day or by night.
Waking or sleeping, Thy presence my light.

Focus on the second line. Try to **put** it into your own words. It could be something like, 'I don't want anything to mean as much to me as you, God'.

```
re:action
```

Now **focus** on the last phrase. **Think** about God bringing light into your life.

Next spend some time **praising God** together in whatever ways are appropriate to the group. This could involve singing, or listening to praise music, reading a psalm of praise aloud, or praying.

Afterwards, **go back** to the newspaper stories you looked at earlier and have everyone choose one to **pray** for. You could do this in a time of open prayer, or you could give everyone time to write down a one- or two-sentence prayer about the story they chose. Then go round the group reading out your prayers in turn.

4 When darkness falls

*You, too, have proved to be of no help.
You have seen my calamity, and you are afraid.*

Job 6:21

set the scene

Everyone should fill in this fun quiz: *How good are you at expressing your feelings?*

1 You're really upset about something but you've got to go into work. Do you:
   a keep disappearing off to the toilets to cry and encourage everyone to assume you're feeling ill?
   b cry on everyone's shoulder and disrupt the whole place for the whole day?
   c hold it all in? You'd never let anyone at work see you were upset about anything.
   d don't mention it to anyone but spend the day snapping at everyone who comes near?
   e upset? What's that?

2 You've won a round the world trip in a competition and you're really excited! Do you:
   a ring up everyone you know and spend hours telling them all about it?
   b mention it casually, in passing, every five minutes all day for weeks?
   c carry on as normal – what's the big deal?
   d tell a few close friends and family, otherwise keep it quiet for now?
   e throw a wild party?

3 Your best friend has passed on a confidence you shared with them and you feel really let down. Do you:

re:action

   a   punch them on the nose and never speak to them again?
   b   disappear to lick your wounds and let them come and find you?
   c   decide that if they're really sorry, you'll give them another chance, but they'd better do a lot of apologising first?
   d   don't mention you know about it but be cool towards them and make snappy remarks and snide asides whenever you're with them?
   e   it couldn't happen because you never tell anyone anything they could use to hurt you?

4 You're really fed up. A friend has bought the expensive designer top you've been eyeing for ages. Worse still they look far better in it than you ever could! Do you:
   a   say you'll hate them forever if they do it again but manage to tell them they look wonderful and mean it?
   b   tell them how great they look as you spill indelible ink down them 'by mistake'?
   c   cheer yourself up with an even more expensive top?
   d   go and cry in the cupboard?
   e   sulk without explaining why?

5 The computer has gone wrong again, trashing your day's work. Do you:
   a   kick it, then throw it away and buy a new one?
   b   smile; you've always been told to smile in the face of adversity!
   c   pretend it doesn't matter but be really nasty to the next person who speaks to you?
   d   burst into tears and hope that someone else will come and sort it out for you?
   e   count to ten, then fix it calmly?

Share your answers with one another and then decide who expresses their feelings most effectively. Discuss what is good about the way they express their feelings.

Next, five minutes or so of quiet to answer these questions on your own:

for the tough times

Q: Is the way you express feelings helpful or not? Why/why not?

Q: What benefits come from sharing your feelings with other people?

Q: What are the risks of doing that?

explore

1 Painful lives

Job had to live with bereavement and ill health. Then there was the loss of his job, income and social status. He didn't know why all this was happening to him. He didn't know what would happen in the future.

Q: Why do you think we commend people who suffer 'bravely' or in stoic silence? (You might never have known anything was wrong with her... he never complained...)

Reality check Screaming at everyone who comes near you; complaining constantly; being utterly obnoxious... none of these might be the best way to communicate feelings with those around you. However, by suggesting that silence is something to be commended – even among a person's close friends and family, even with God – we may imply that their fears and feelings are too hot for anyone to handle, leaving them to be faced alone.

For the next question, you might like to split into three smaller groups, each tackling one of the sections. After discussion one person from each group can summarise the group's discoveries for the rest.

Q: How did Job feel...
about his own life?

Read
Job 3:11–17; 6:8–13; 7:13–16.

re:action

about the people around him?
Read
Job 6:14–17; 19:13–22

about God?
Read
Job 23:11–17; 30:16–23

Job did not hang back in his conversations with his friends and with God. He didn't bottle up his feelings or keep these thoughts inside his head. Instead he told it exactly as it felt.

He wasn't the only one to do so; David is another Bible character who also spoke to God with raw honesty:

My God, my God! Why have you forsaken me?
  Why do you remain so distant?
  Why do you ignore my cries for help?

Psalm 22:1

I am worn out from sobbing.
  Every night tears drench my bed;
my pillow is wet from weeping.
  My vision is blurred by grief;
  my eyes are worn out because of all my enemies.

Psalm 6:6,7

Q: How did God respond to Job's blunt speaking? Check out Job 38:1–3; 42:7,8.

Q: What do you think God didn't like about Job's speeches?

Q: And what did he see as right?

for the tough times

This next quotation is from best-selling American author Philip Yancey, in his book *The Bible Jesus Read:*

God prefers honest disagreement to dishonest submission. He takes human beings seriously, conducts dialogues with them, includes them in his plans, listens to them.

Q: Do you agree with Yancey?

Q: Why do you think God put up with Job's anger and complaints towards him?

Q: Why do we sometimes fear that speaking our mind to God is wrong?

reflect

Sometimes it can be hard to admit we are in pain even to ourselves and to God. Spend some minutes in quiet, considering the next few challenging questions on your own.

Q: How honest are you when you speak to God?

Q: Why is it important to be honest with him?

Q: And how honest are you when you speak to other people?

Q: Why is it important to be honest with one another?

Q: Are there areas of your life where you aren't being honest? Is there a first step you could take to change that this week?

Think about whether it would be helpful for the rest of the group to pray specifically for you about this. If you decide it would be, you could ask for prayer during the re:action time.

re:action

Distribute some small pieces of paper or card. Everyone should **write** a different feeling (eg happy, miserable, excited) on about half a dozen pieces each. Then each person looks at their collection, and **selects** one that matches their current feeling about some situation they would like the group to **pray** for. It could be something personal, some situation known to them, or something from the wider world.

Each person **explains** the prayer need and their feeling about it before praying together. This can be done silently or out loud. If there's time, you could all choose a second or even third feeling and a different prayer need.

As well as your own choices of prayer needs, try to remember at least one other person's prayer needs from the group and **continue to pray** for them during the week. When you next meet, take the opportunity of asking the person if God has yet answered or begun to answer that particular need. Express your gratitude for any answered prayers by reporting God's response to the whole group.

5 Facing pain

When they heard of the tragedy he had suffered, they got together and travelled from their homes to comfort and console him.

Job 2:11b

set the scene

Q: Which of these statements is true for you? Tick those that are.

____ I have lots of good friends.
____ I have lots of acquaintances.
____ I have a small number of very close friends.
____ I make friends easily.
____ I like to be around lots of people.
____ I like spending time with the same few people.
____ I find it hard to build deep friendships.
____ I wish I had more good friends.
____ I am happy with the friends I have.
____ I am a good friend to have.

Discuss the following questions:
Q: What changes an acquaintance into a friend?

Q: And a friend into a close friend?

Q: What qualities make a really good friend?

re:action

1 Coping with other people's pain

Read
Job 2:11–13

Q: When Job's friends came to visit, how did they first respond to his distress?

Q: Do you think this was a good way to help Job or not?

Once Job started to speak about his feelings, his friends began to speak too.

Read
Job 6:21–30, 16:1–5 and 19:1–6

Q: What did Job want from his friends?

Q: What did he actually get?

Job's friends tried to come up with a reason for his suffering (his sinfulness) and suggested ways to overcome it. The essence of what Eliphaz had to say was:

Stop quarrelling with God! If you agree with him, you will have peace at last, and things will go well for you. Listen to his instructions, and store them in your heart.

Job 22:21,22

And this was at the heart of what Bildad advised:

…if you pray to God and seek the favour of the Almighty, if you are pure and live with complete integrity, he will rise up and restore your happy home.

Job 8:5,6

for the tough times

While Zophar's suggestion was:

If only you would prepare your heart and lift up your hands to him in prayer! Get rid of your sins and leave all iniquity behind you. Then your face will brighten in innocence. You will be strong and free of fear.
Job 11:13–15

Q: What did these men say would help Job's situation? What do you think of their ideas?

Reality check We often offer people quick-fix responses to their suffering. How often do you hear, or say:

Look on the bright side; count your blessings!
There's always someone worse off than you.
If you had enough faith, then God would heal you.
Pray, and God will work it all out for you.

It takes a whole load of things such as courage, self-control and maturity to face pain with honesty. Often other people's reactions don't help at all. For instance, ignoring people's problems doesn't make them go away, and neither does doling out platitudes.

2 Can everything be fixed? If I had more faith, would everything be alright?

In his gospel Matthew describes many occasions when Jesus healed people.

Read
Matthew 8:5–13 and 9:1–8

Q: Who was healed in these stories?

Q: Whose faith was commended?

Reality check When Jesus healed people, the outcome wasn't solely dependent on the faith of the person who was ill. John tells us of a man healed at the Pool of Bethesda who didn't even know who Jesus

re:action

was (John 5:1–15). Sometimes no one had any faith in Jesus' power to change things at all. When Lazarus was dead, everyone believed Jesus had come too late – but he went ahead and raised him anyway (John 11:17–44).

3 But can everything be fixed? What if I had prayed more?

Jesus did not want to suffer on the cross:

Father, if you are willing, please take this cup of suffering away from me...
Luke 22:42

But he did suffer.

Q: What do you think? Either:

- Jesus didn't pray enough
- Jesus didn't pray with enough faith
- prayer does not guarantee that God will protect us or relieve our suffering

Paul too prayed for relief from suffering – but didn't always receive it. Speaking about the (unidentified) thorn in the flesh he says:

Three different times I begged the Lord to take it away...
2 Corinthians 12:8

reflect

Job's friends, and many people in the church today, seek easy answers to the problem of suffering. That's not to say we shouldn't pray faithfully for relief from suffering for others and ourselves. Jesus and Paul prayed for help, believing in God's power to change things and sometimes he did. However, Jesus, Paul and Job show us there is **often no direct link** between something a person does (or doesn't do) and what happens to them.

Q: Why do you think people are so keen to create and trust in such links?

for the tough times

When a person in pain speaks honestly about their feelings, expressing their fears, doubts and anger, it can be hard for the hearer to cope. They may even respond with anger or dismissal.

Q: Why do you think people sometimes react so strongly when they hear such feelings expressed?

Q: Have you experienced someone sharing strong emotions with you?

Q: How did you respond?

Q: What might help us to listen to other people's pain more effectively?

There are no quick solutions to our experiences of suffering, just as there weren't for Job.

Q: What do you think are the best ways to help someone in pain?

It can be costly for those supporting someone who is in deep distress. It can be very hard to sit beside someone who is suffering and know you can't change what is happening to them.

Q: How can we support the supporters, too?

re:action

Imagine you have faced the kind of disasters that overcame Job. Your family are all gone. Where would you turn for help? And what kind of hope would you be looking for?

Pray together, giving thanks for the people you know you could turn to in times of real trouble. And then **pray** for people known to you who are struggling with illness, troubled relationships, difficulties at home or at work, finances, tough decisions, anxieties about the future.

```
re:action
```

If you have experienced any kind of support from someone recently, why not **ring** them or **send** them a card to thank them this week, even if you have expressed this before? Or, if you know someone who is having a hard time, you could **ring** them or **send** them a card to encourage them, or offer your support if they need it.

You could end your time by **reading** to each other this personalised blessing from 2 Corinthians 13:14:

May the grace of our Lord Jesus Christ, the love of God, and the fellowship of the Holy Spirit be with us all.

for the tough times

6 God's response

> ...you have not been right in what you said about me, as my servant Job was.
>
> **Job 42:7**

set the scene

Everyone in the group should write down their answers to these three questions on pieces of paper. You may want to try and disguise your handwriting if you think it will be recognised by others in the group!

1. What is your favourite food?
2. What's your favourite method of transport?
3. What's the best film you've ever seen?

Collect up the answers, jumble them up and then have one person read out each set of answers in turn. As they do that, the rest write down whose answers they think they are. At the end, get each person to reveal the truth.

(If your group know each other very well and it seems likely that identities will be easy to guess, make up some different questions.)

explore

1 God's answer

In chapters 38–41, God finally responds to Job's complaints and requests for information.

As examples of God's replies:

Read
Job 38:1–18
Job 41:1–11

Q: How would you sum up God's response to Job?

re:action

God's reply to Job is perhaps most notable for what it leaves out.

Q: Why do you think God never even mentions Job's suffering?

Read
Job 42:1–6

Q: How does Job then respond to God?

Q: What kind of feelings does Job have about God now?

Q: What is he repenting for?

Job knew God as the awesome creator, the 'Fear of Isaac' as Jacob describes him in Genesis 31:42.

Can you shout to the clouds and make it rain?
Can you make lightning appear
and cause it to strike as you direct it?
Job 38:34,35

Job submitted to God, acknowledging his power and his right to do as he pleased with his creation, clinging onto his faith in him.

2 The vulnerable Creator

For us, he is that same awe-inspiring God, the all-powerful Creator. But he is more. We know the vulnerable man that he became.

And while they were there, the time came for her baby to be born. She gave birth to her first child, a son. She wrapped him snugly in strips of cloth and laid him in a manger, because there was no room for them in the village inn.
Luke 2:6,7

Q: Do you find it easier to think of God as the holy and awesome Creator or as the man Jesus?

for the tough times

Q: How does that affect your understanding of the way God works?

Q: What elements of God's character does Jesus show us?

Like Job we have to decide whether God is worth following whatever happens to us. Unlike Job we don't just have to take it on trust that God loves us and understands our problems. In Jesus we see that he does; he shows us how God responds to us and to the problems of life.

Q: What kinds of suffering and difficulties did Jesus experience? Spend a few minutes identifying them and list them alongside the Bible references:

John 7:1
John 11:32–35
Mark 14:32–35
Luke 22:48,57–60
Luke 22:63–65

Reality check Jesus experienced life as we do, with the **same** powerlessness and feelings of abandonment by God. Jesus means that God understands what it is like to be me.

3 Future justice

Not everyone who suffers receives physical healing or restoration in this life. Most of the disciples and Paul suffered and went on to meet unpleasant deaths. Many others also suffered without relief.

Read
Revelation 20:11–21:4

Q: What will happen to those who now deny God?

Q: And to those who trust in him?

re:action

In the darkness of his suffering, Job wanted to die. Paul too says,

We were crushed and completely overwhelmed, and we thought we would never live through it. In fact, we expected to die.
2 Corinthians 1:8b,9a

When we experience suffering, the prospect of heaven – with no more pain and tears – can seem hugely attractive. Some, like Job, may wish for death rather than have to carry on living.

Q: How can the hope of heaven be an encouragement to endure the difficult times of life, rather than seen as our only hope of release?

reflect

On the cross Jesus experienced the feeling of being abandoned by God. Job too felt abandoned to his fate by God.

I cry out for help, but no one hears me. I protest but there is no justice.
Job 19:7

Turn back to the **Intro** and read what C S Lewis wrote about searching for God and feeling as if he came up against a closed door.

Q: Have you experienced the feeling of God going missing just when you really need him?

Q: Do you think God's silence meant that he had left Job (or Jesus) to struggle alone?

Elihu reminds Job that even when we can't feel him near us, God still speaks to us.

But God speaks again and again, though people do not recognise it.
Job 33:14

Q: When God seems very far away, how might he still be speaking to us?

for the tough times

Further in his book *A Grief Observed*, C S Lewis has more to say about the bolted door slammed in his face:

I have gradually been coming to feel that the door is no longer shut and bolted. Was it my own frantic need that slammed it in my face? The time when there is nothing at all in your soul except a cry for help may be just the time when God can't give it: you are like the drowning man who can't be helped because he clutches and grabs. Perhaps your own reiterated cries deafen you to the voice you hoped to hear.

Q: Do you think he has a point or not?

Q: What has helped you cope during times when God has been silent?

God's silence encouraged Job to think that he (God) was not concerned with his problems. For us there can be certainty that God always loves us even when life seems very tough – because of Jesus.

Read
Matthew 9:36
John 11:32–35
Luke 13:34
John 15:12,13

Q: Just pure speculation, but how might Job's response to his suffering have changed if he had known Jesus?

re:action

Think again about the question you tackled on page 37 about what elements of God's character Jesus shows us.

From an A4 sheet of paper or card everyone should **cut** out the four corners to leave a cross shape. **Pool** your answers to this question and **write** them onto your crosses. **Hold** your cross as you **pray together**, **thanking** God for Jesus and the difference he makes to your life. You might like to **choose** one characteristic that makes a special impact on

re:action

you in some way.

Read together Philippians 2:5–11:

Your attitude should be the same that Christ Jesus had. Though he was God, he did not demand and cling to his rights as God. He made himself nothing; he took the humble position of a slave and appeared in human form. And in human form he obediently humbled himself even further by dying a criminal's death on a cross. Because of this, God raised him up to the heights of heaven and gave him a name that is above every other name, so that at the name of Jesus every knee will bow, in heaven and on earth and under the earth, and every tongue will confess that Jesus Christ is Lord, to the glory of God the Father.

You could go on using your cross as you pray this week.

7 But it still hurts...

> *He knows where I am going.*
> *And when he has tested me like gold in a fire,*
> *he will pronounce me innocent.*
>
> **Job 23:10**

set the scene

Q: Do you like happy endings? Why?

Q: Have you ever watched a film or read a book when the ending seemed completely wrong for the story? Describe it to the group and talk about how you felt.

Q: Does your frame of mind (happy, sad, tired, stressed...) alter the kind of things you like to watch and read?

Q: What would you choose when you were really happy? Or stressed? Or sad?

explore

1 Happy endings

For the three friends, Eliphaz, Bildad and Zophar, the story ends with God's anger, redeemed only by Job's prayers. For Job it ends with his life restored.

When Job prayed for his friends, the Lord restored his fortunes. In fact the Lord gave him twice as much as before!

re:action

So the Lord blessed Job in the second half of his life even more than in the beginning.
Job 42:10,12a

Q: Why do you think God gave Job back so much?

Some might say that Job's experience shows that those who hold onto faith in difficult times will be really blessed in the end.

Read
Hebrews 11:32–38

Here we see some people being saved from disaster – and others not. All were commended for their faith but not all received the same end. We know that God does see people suffering and often steps in to sort it out. Some are healed, or freed from various kinds of prisons, even restored to life. But his intervention is not predictable. It doesn't always remove our problems.

Q: If God loves us why doesn't he always step in and make it better?

Q: How do you feel when you see someone suffering and God doesn't step in and sort it out?

Reality check Part of the answer seems to lie in the truth that the very nature of life is to be unfair and unpredictable; bad things do happen to good people. However, there seem to be other factors too. Miracles, for example – events that by definition are unusual, defying our expectations.

Read
John 2:11; 6:14; 9:24–34; 11:38–44

Q: Why did Jesus perform miracles?

Q: What did his miracles show people?

for the tough times

Jesus performed miracles for a purpose, to show people who he was. By doing so, he forced them to make a decision, to follow him or not. However, it wasn't just Jesus who did miracles.

Read
Acts 9:39–42

Q: What happened because Tabitha was raised?

Read
Acts 14:1–3

Q: Why did God enable Paul and Barnabas to work miracles?

Read
Acts 16:25–32

Q: Why was the prison destroyed?

God works miracles, not just to benefit the person or people involved, but as a sign for them and others. That sign points to him, showing how life was meant to be and one day will be:

He will remove all of their sorrows, and there will be no more death or sorrow or crying or pain. For the old world and its evils have gone for ever.
Revelation 21:4

Read
1 Peter 1:3–7

Q: What does Peter suggest is God's priority for his people?

Reality check So? God does not always take away our troubles, even though at times he does deal in the out-of-the-ordinary, the supernatural, the miraculous. However, his aim is not primarily to help us feel good but to develop faith in him.

2 God at work through you and me

Read
Ephesians 2:19–22

Q: Who are we?

Being a member of the body of Christ is not just about being part of a club where everyone knows God's forgiveness and new life. With our experience of God's grace and mercy come responsibilities to one another.

Q: What kind of responsibilities do we have towards each other? Share your thoughts and then check out these Bible verses. You might like to list your findings alongside.

Read
1 John 3:16–20
Colossians 3:12–17
Ephesians 4:25
Galatians 6:2
Luke 6:37–38

Jesus is no longer on earth as a man, flesh and blood that we can touch, providing comfort by his physical presence. Now Jesus uses his body, the church, to carry out that role in the world.

Philip Yancey sums up our responsibility when he says,

'Where is God when it hurts?' I have often asked. The answer is in another question, 'Where is the church when it hurts?'
from *The Jesus I Never Knew*

Reality check Much suffering would be greatly lessened if the church – you and me – were really expressing Jesus' love to one another.

Q: How can we live out our responsibilities to one another more effectively?

3 Good out of suffering

Read

Romans 5:3–5
2 Corinthians 12:8–10

Q: What good things did Paul learn through his experiences of suffering?

Q: Do you agree with this, written by Paul to the early church in Rome?

And we know that God causes everything to work together for the good of those who love God and are called according to his purpose for them.
Romans 8:28.

reflect

Take a few minutes of silence to look back on your life and see if you can identify any time when God really did bring good out of an experience of difficulty and suffering. Or was there a specific bad experience that later equipped you to be helpful and useful to someone else going through a tough time? You may be able to share some of this with the group.

Summary:

We have seen that Satan causes a person's suffering, not God, though he can only do so by God's permission. Even in the darkest situations there is hope. God can bring some good out of everything that happens to us, even though it may only become obvious to us much later.

There are no absolute answers or easy answers to many of the big questions about suffering. It's one of those issues that probably we will never understand completely, though through wrestling with our experiences and with the truths of the Bible we will pick up some clues along the way.

Difficult as the questions might be, we are not called to be resigned to suffering, but to challenge it. Though it is a natural part of our world for now, God's true intention for us does not include suffering. It is not unreasonable that in the tough times we may question our faith and argue with God. We may feel that God is far away and have great need of the support of others to bring us through dark times. However, just as God transformed the suffering of Jesus into triumph on Easter morning, so there is hope that our own troubles can one day be transformed too.

Q: How much do you agree with this summary?

Think again about Job's experience.

Q: Is Job's story really about **why** we suffer?

Even late on in the book when God speaks directly to Job, he doesn't answer the question why. Should we say that Job is rather about our **response** to suffering and hardship? Job has to decide whether he trusts God solely because of the good things he has received from him, or whether his faith is based on something stronger than that. We need to face the same question.

Q: Is your faith dependent on receiving and experiencing good things from God?

Q: Has your faith ever been really tested by tough times?

Q: How did you get through those times? Are there lessons your experiences taught you that will help you care for others who are suffering now?

re:action

Think about ways in which these group times have helped you to understand more about suffering.

If someone in the group made a note at the **Preview** meeting of the

for the tough times

insights the group was looking for, now's the time to get that out and **discuss** how far those ambitions were achieved. Talk about how prepared you feel to face future tough times.

Talk over future plans for the group. Are you continuing to meet, with new materials to guide your discussions and study? Or taking a break and re-forming as a group later?

Pray for one another, particularly those in the middle of tough experiences right now.

The hymn we've already mentioned, *Be Thou my Vision*, ends with these words:

Heart of my own heart, whatever befall,
Still be my Vision, O Ruler of all.

Use these words as a group as you **re-commit** yourselves to serving Jesus – whatever life may bring. You could do this through a few minutes of open **prayer**, through **writing** individual letters to Jesus, by praying a prayer of commitment together such as that found in the booklet *Journey into Life*, or simply by **singing** together the whole of the hymn.

Re:action small group Bible resources by Kate Hayes

Others in the series

Jesus: the sequel
Is he really coming back?
Appointments, schedules, timetables ... we live in a time-bound society. It's so easy to live just for the present. Are you ready for the future? Not just your next career move... your next property... your next set of wheels... or even your plans for retirement. But the future that begins when Jesus himself returns!
ISBN 1 85999 621 3

Chosen for change
Am I part of God's big plan?
Like it or not, you're living in the 'me' culture. Are you comfortable with going it alone, taking care of 'Number One', cashing in on 'your rights' and turning a blind eye to responsibilities? What about sharing... caring... belonging... teamwork... community? Are you ready to serve not self – but society?
ISBN 1 85999 623 X

The possibility of purpose
What's the meaning of my life?
A treadmill existence of deadlines and pressures? Or a kaleidoscope of amazing opportunities? What's your take on daily life? Do you see yourself as a meaningless cosmic dust speck? Or a significant mover in a masterplan? Your view affects your motivation, your self-esteem, your priorities, your everyday choices...
ISBN 1 85999 620 5

Available from all good Christian bookshops *or*
- phone SU's mail order line: 01908 856006
- email info@scriptureunion.org.uk
- fax 01908 856020
- log on to www.scriptureunion.org.uk
- or write to SU Mail Order:
  PO Box 5148, Milton Keynes MLO, MK2 2YX